MIDLOTHIAN
PUBLIC LIBRARY

USING MONEY

AT THE LEMONADE STAND

Please visit our web site at: www.garethstevens.com
For a free color catalog describing our list of high-quality books,
call 1-800-542-2595 (USA) or 1-800-387-3178 (Canada).

Library of Congress Cataloging-in-Publication Data

Rauen, Amy.
    Using money at the lemonade stand / Amy Ayers — North American ed.
      p. cm. — (Math in our world)
    ISBN-13: 978-0-8368-8472-2 (lib. bdg.)
    ISBN-10: 0-8368-8472-8 (lib. bdg.)
    ISBN-13: 978-0-8368-8481-4 (softcover)
    ISBN-10: 0-8368-8481-7 (softcover)
    1. Counting—Juvenile literature. 2. Money—Juvenile literature. I. Title.
QA113.A94   2007
513.2'11—dc22   2007017949

This edition first published in 2008 by
Weekly Reader® Books
An imprint of Gareth Stevens Publishing
1 Reader's Digest Road
Pleasantville, NY 10570-7000 USA

Copyright © 2008 by Gareth Stevens, Inc.

Managing editor: Dorothy L. Gibbs
Art direction: Tammy West

Photo credits: All photographs by Russell Pickering, except p. 8 © H.G. Rossi/Zefa/Corbis;
pp. 10, 12 © Myrleen Ferguson Cate/Photo Edit; p. 13 © Dennis Degnan/Corbis.

Printed in the United States of America

1 2 3 4 5 6 7 8 9 11 10 09 08 07

USING MONEY
AT THE LEMONADE STAND

by Amy Rauen

Photographs by Russell Pickering

Reading consultant: Susan Nations, M.Ed., author/
literacy coach/consultant in literacy development

Math consultant: Rhea Stewart, M.A., mathematics content specialist

WEEKLY READER®
PUBLISHING

My brother and I set up a lemonade
stand. It is by our house.

We want to earn money. We will use
the money to buy our sister a present.

Small Lemonade
25¢

We will sell small and large servings of lemonade. The small serving costs 25¢.

Large Lemonade
45¢

The large serving costs 45¢.

Here are our mom and sister.

Large
Lemonade
45¢

25¢   35¢   45¢

Mom buys a large serving of lemonade.
The large cup costs 45¢.

Here come Luis and Roberto. They are with their dad.

Small
Lemonade
25¢

25¢   50¢   75¢

They buy three small servings of lemonade.
Each small cup costs 25¢. Three small
cups cost 75¢ in all.

Now I see my teacher and her little girl.
Uncle Dave and Aunt Patty are here, too.

12

Here come the twins from next door! We also see our friends Nicki and Kendra. What a line!

5¢

10¢

15¢

20¢

25¢

Small
Lemonade

25¢

My teacher buys one small serving of
lemonade. The small cup costs 25¢.

Large
Lemonade
45¢

25¢   50¢   75¢

85¢   90¢

Uncle Dave and Aunt Patty buy two large servings. Each large cup costs 45¢. Two large cups cost 90¢ in all.

The twins buy two small servings.
Each small cup costs 25¢. Two
small cups cost 50¢ in all.

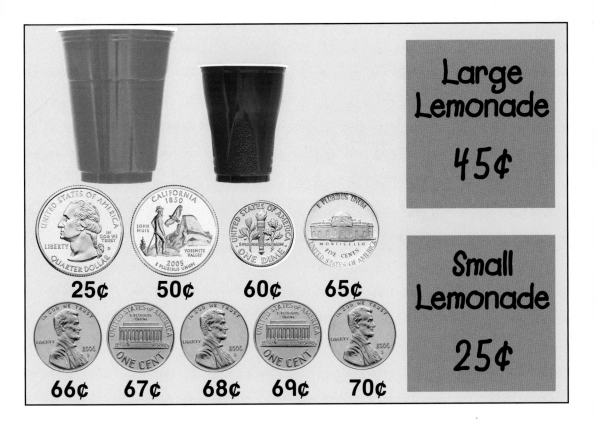

Large
Lemonade

45¢

Small
Lemonade

25¢

25¢   50¢   60¢   65¢

66¢   67¢   68¢   69¢   70¢

Nicki and Kendra buy one large serving and one small serving. One large cup and one small cup cost 70¢ in all.

Soon, it is time to clean up. Dad asks us to wait. He says one more person wants lemonade.

My brother and I look around. We do not
see anyone.

Then we look at Dad. He has coins.
Dad wants lemonade!

Large
Lemonade

45¢

25¢   35¢   40¢

41¢   42¢   43¢   44¢   45¢

Dad buys a large serving for 45¢. Now we
are out of lemonade.

My brother and I close our lemonade
stand. We count our money.

We earned enough money to buy our
sister a present!

Glossary

coin – a special piece of metal that is used for money

lemonade – a drink made from lemon juice and water

lemonade stand – a place to buy lemonade

present – a gift that someone gives to you or that you give to someone

About the Author

Amy Rauen is the author of thirteen math books for children. She also designs and writes educational software. Amy lives in San Diego, California, with her husband and their two cats.